"For the millions of women who suffer from Paris envy, *Chic in Paris* is a guide to unveiling the French fashion enigma. This guide consists of interviews with eight Parisian women whom I have selected for their undisputed taste in fashion, their sense of self that is expressed in their style philosophy, and their secret addresses of boutiques, couturiers and designers that allows them to pull it all inimitably together. If 'style' is about personal expression, and fashion its vehicle, it is certainly the successful blending of the two in which Parisian women excel. They know who they are, and where to get what they need to convey their essence with brio. The secret, therefore, lies in the right mix of personality and product."

CHIC
IN PARIS

STYLE SECRETS & BEST ADDRESSES

Susan Tabak

What is it about Paris and Parisian women that embodies the word "style"? How is it that *la femme parisienne*, no matter what her age or body shape, displays a sense of self and a sense of being a woman that is missing elsewhere in the world? What gives real, everyday French women that *je ne sais quoi* perfect look whether they're in the boardroom, the boudoir, the sidewalk café, or the after-hours jazz club? And just where do they get the abilility to appear simultaneously smart and sexy with a seemingly effortless combination of elegance, grace, and classic chic?

Chic in Paris unlocks this mystery for the many women who wish that they too, could appear as coolly confident as their Parisian counterparts. For the first time, readers will discover the real style secrets of the City of Light, revealed through luminous photography accompanied by insider insights and observations, along with practical tips for bringing Parisian style home. The author makes it her business to know the *ins* and *outs* of the most exciting places to shop in the world's greatest city. She knows both the chicest shops and those that are off the beaten path. *Chic in Paris* reveals some of the hottest spots in the City of Light.

BOU

Pari

I was born and raised in Paris in the Sixties. Since then, I have never left without a return ticket. I love Paris. Kiraz, Christian Dior, François Truffaut, Micheline Presle, Sacha Guitry have all, in their own way, celebrated La Parisienne. La Parisienne is not labeled as blonde or brunette, a career woman or a lady of leisure. Her voice is important and she carries her allure with a certain nonchalance, which answers for her natural elegance. From Worth at the beginning of the 20th century, to Yves Saint Laurent, Paris has always been the nest for Fashion and Couture. So, La Parisienne has always had her choice, it is in her genes. With the immense variety of shops, jewelers, couturiers, designers, cobblers, she never needs to look elsewhere to look good. Like a butterfly fluttering from flower to flower, she picks here and there that which will make her look fabulous. She is unfaithful to fashion and its designers. This is why she can remain faithful to something much more important: her style. Through my work I have always tried to respect that choice. "Tall and tan and young and lovely"…One song, "The Girl from Ipanema", speaks so clearly of La Parisienne that I sometimes wish that the alteration of one single word would make it instead a hymn to Loulou, Nathalie, Georgina, Mina… She, La Parisienne, is all of them.

Christian Louboutin

Georgina
Brandolini

I had the pleasure of meeting Georgina at a dinner party at Valentino's home outside of Paris. Georgina's long hair and understated style give her a look of perpetual youth. You might even say that her love of dressing in jeans and sweaters gives her an American style, but her cool, confident manner offers a distinctly European allure. She has a fascinating background: born in Rio de Janeiro to a French Prince and a Brazilian Lady, she is a Parisian Countess who married an Italian nobleman and industrialist. After 22 years as Valentino's muse and brilliant press attaché, Georgina joined Balmain as an executive and managed the prêt-à-porter for six years. Following this, she decided to launch her own line of knitwear and in November 2005, opened her first Parisian boutique on the boulevard Raspail. Her knitwear, which reflects her no-nonsense, straightforward manner, brings a casual approach to chic by mixing cashmere, silk, and embroidery. Complemented by other products such as handbags, jeans, and jackets, the spirit of her collection is dressy yet relaxed, sophisticated in its simplicity.

Personal style &
style *philosophy*

Georgina, with all this exposure to fashion, what do you think defines French style and distinguishes it from others? I think French style is very tailored.

How would you define your personal style, and what outside influences impact your style sense? My personal style, influenced by Italian fashion, tends to be sporty and casual, yet sophisticated.

Is there such a thing as good and bad taste when it comes to style?
Good taste means wearing what feels comfortable and knowing that it goes with your own personal style. That's what makes you look great!

What in your opinion is the biggest fashion *faux pas*?
To wear the latest trend when it does not suit you.

What is your signature look?
Jeans and sweaters.

How do you dress for a last-minute special occasion?
I always have a pair of jeans or black pants in my drawer that I can wear with one of my evening sweaters.

"Do you have any tips to having style? *Wear what you feel good in even if it is not the latest fashion.*"

My personal *style* tends to be sporty and casual yet *sophisticated.*

Fashion & *accessories*

Which designer best reflects your personal style?
Valentino, because he is my mentor. He taught me everything I know and I've worked with him for 20 years. I think he makes women look beautiful, chic, and sexy.

What are your signature accessories? Do they change from day to night?
A lovely handbag can make your look completely different, which is great when you want to travel light.

Who is your favorite shoe designer?
Christian Louboutin designs great, trendy high heels. For sandals, Miu Miu designs fantastic flats' with stones.

And for handbags? Valentino bags are the most glamorous for evening, Chloé is perfect for daytime, and Fendi bags are the most striking.

What are your three must-have wardrobe pieces?
A black tuxedo jacket, a long skirt, a pair of dark jeans, and all of my sweaters, of course.

What was your last great fashion discovery?
Embroideries in Nepal, short, printed dresses, that everybody is designing now and Chloé boots with high high-heels. These are the best because they are actually comfortable.

Are there any tips for having great style?
Wear what you feel good in, even if it is not the latest fashion.

Beauty

Who is your hairdresser of choice? Alexandre Zouari.

What is your morning beauty ritual?
I love to spray some Evian water on my face.

What are your favorite beauty products?
Estée Lauder Night Repair and Khiel's for day and night.

What aspects of your health-beauty regime could you not live without?

My Thaï massage and *Pilates lessons.*

Do you have a signature scent, and does it change with the seasons?
I have been using Eau du Soir de Sisley for a long time, and in the summer I use Eau Sauvage by Dior.

What small personal pleasure do you treat yourself to occasionally?
A good skin cleansing at Alexandre Zouari in Paris, or in Brazil where they are the best.

What is the best beauty advice you have been given?
Not to drink or smoke.

Lifestyle

Do you have a preferred style of interior home design?

I have a lot of contemporary pictures on the wall and use very clear fabrics, white if possible. I like there to be lots of clean space but I also like a cozy atmosphere so I have very comfortable sofas and armchairs.

What elements create your personal ambiance at home?

I love my orchids and my Georgina Brandolini candles.

In your home, which is the most important room for you and why?

My bedroom, where my children and husband always come and where we all watch television, talk, and sometimes eat.

Which are your favorite restaurants?

Le Voltaire is very good and very fashionable. Mathis is fun at night and always has an eclectic group of people. L'Entrecôte is very good and quick and has the best French fries and sauce. Le Stresa has very good pasta and good-looking ladies who "lunch." Le Moulin à Vent has very good typical French food, bistro-style.

Le Voltaire is very good and very *fashionable*

Loulou
de la Falaise

Anyone exposed to the world of art and fashion reveres and admires Loulou de la Falaise. Born in England and raised in Paris and London, Loulou entered the fashion world as a model for Vogue and a fabric designer for Halston in New York. In 1972, she joined the House of Yves Saint Laurent and began an amazing 30-year relationship with one of the world's most influential designers, acting as both his muse and chief creative consultant. In 2003, she opened her own two-floor boutique at 7 rue de Bourgogne and shifted from creative advisor to full-fledged designer. Loulou's clothes are made for the modern woman who wants old-style sophistication but does not want to look old-fashioned. Loulou is not afraid of color or fabric. She mixes silks with woolens, cashmere, and tulle. When you shop in her boutiques on the rue de Bourgogne or the rue Cambon, you know you are truly in Paris!

Personal style & style *philosophy*

Loulou, as the fashion icon that you are, what do you think defines French style and distinguishes it from others?

The French are more conventional than other nationalities. They are not as sexy as the Italians or as *habilleés* as the Americans.

How would you define your personal style, and what outside influences impact your style sense?

My personal style is inspired by everyday life, but if I had to label it, I would define it more specifically as "boyish." Fashion and the accessories that I collect influence me.

Is there such a thing as good and bad taste when it comes to style?

Poor taste is simply a lack of imagination - I don't believe in it. Taste is in the eye of the beholder. A fashion faux pas is what happens when you're not confident with yourself.

Do you have a style icon?

My icons are real-life people, who know how to live life and have a good time, Nancy Cunard, for example.

What is your signature look?

I wear colorful clothes, high heels, and bunches of bangles on my wrists.

"My icons are *real-life* people, who know how to live life...

I tend to *find myself mixing and* matching *different* designers.

Fashion &
accessories

Which designer best reflects your personal style?
I tend to find myself mixing and matching different designers.

Who is your favorite shoe designer?
I love Christian Louboutin's shoes because they are by far the sexiest.

And for handbags?
I carry my fox fur handbag all the time. Not only does it hold a lot, it never loses its style or shape.

What are your three must-have wardrobe pieces?
Black skinny trousers, a cashmere V-neck in a bright color, and a black velvet jacket.

What was your last great fashion discovery?
My latest discovery is black jewels in jet, onyx, and other somber-colored stones such as black tourmaline, mixed with bright stones like turquoise, jade, or coral.

Beauty

Who is your hairdresser of choice?
Katia and Valentin, who work as a team and come to my house on a motorbike.

What are your favorite beauty products?
Touche Eclat by Yves Saint Laurent and Eau de Beauté by Caudalie.

Which beauty treatments could you not do without?
Sleep and Nuxe body cream.

Do you have a signature scent?
I tend to mix fragrances in order to obtain an original scent. I like the ones by Floriana.

What do you do for exercise?

I garden, walk a lot, and swim.

Lifestyle

**What elements help create
your personal ambiance at home?**
I love crystal, plants, candles, and colorful
fabrics bought during my travels.

Which are your favorite restaurants?
I like Le Dôme, Le Duc, Café de Flore and
L'Assiette, a bistro next door to me.

Inès
de la Fressange

Inès is a fashion icon I have admired all my life. With short sexy hair and always dressed in slim pants, she embodies chic simplicity. Inès began modeling in 1975. She who thought her legs too thin, her eyes too big, and her hands unattractive went on to become the face of the perfume Coco by Chanel from 1983 to 1989, personifying French beauty and Parisian elegance. In 1991, she created her own fashion and fragrance label which enjoyed immediate international success. In 2004, she began her collaboration with Bruno Frisoni to re-launch the haute couture shoe brand Roger Vivier, for which she is now the Ambassador.

Personal style & style *philosophy*

Ines, as the quintessence of Parisian chic, what do you think defines French style and distinguishes it from others?
French style is unique because it allows great freedom in mixing styles from different designers. French style also implies not being afraid to wear clothes from past seasons and sometimes ignoring what fashion dictates.

What in your opinion is the biggest fashion *faux pas*?
Earrings with huge logos.

Do you have a style icon?   Jane Birkin and Katherine Hepburn for their casual chic.

What is your signature look?
A navy blue blazer worn over jeans with a pair of loafers, nice make-up, clean hair, and a smile. I try not to get bored with clothes so I mix a lot of things and go against conventions. Evening clothes during the day and sneakers in the evening!

"I try not to get bored with clothes so *I mix a lot of things* and go against *conventions.*"

Fashion &
accessories

Which designer most reflects your personal style?
I buy clothes, not labels. Nevertheless, I find that Jean Paul Gaultier cuts jackets very well, as Chloé does pants. I also like Vanessa Bruno.

What are your signature accessories? Do they change from day to night?
Handbags. One should change them all the time.

What are you favorite handbag brands?
The Hermès Kelly handbag is always fun.

And for shoes?
Roger Vivier on rue du Faubourg Saint-Honoré.

Jewelry designers?
Barboza, located at the corner of rue de Castiglione and rue Saint-Honoré. They specialize in refined antique jewelry. You can find very unique 19th century pieces, either in precious, semi-precious, or volcanic stones, as well as other rarities at very good prices.

What are your three must-have wardrobe pieces?
A pair of Belle Vivier ballerinas with buckles, Chloé pants, and knitwear from Prada and Zadig et Voltaire.

A pair of *Belle Vivier* ballerinas with buckle, Chloé pants, and knitwear from Prada and *Zadig et Voltaire.*

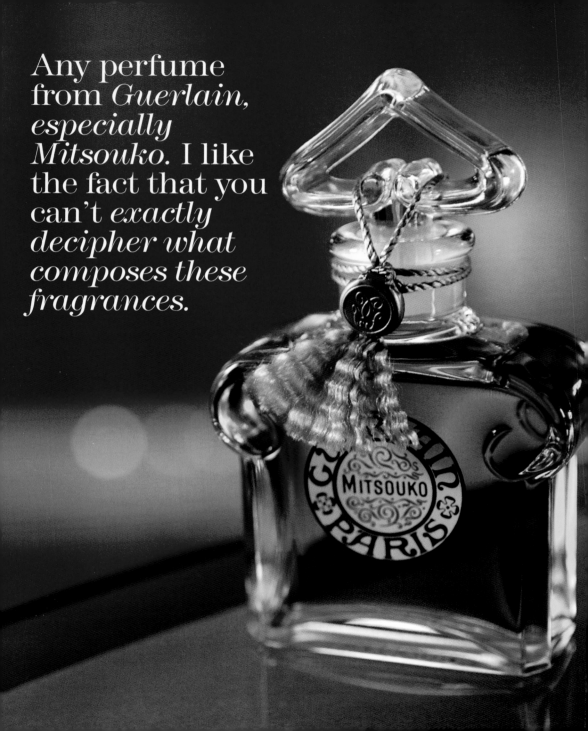

Any perfume from *Guerlain,* especially *Mitsouko.* I like the fact that you can't *exactly decipher what composes these fragrances.*

Beauty

Who is your hairdresser of choice?
Katia, she goes with me everywhere. Once your hair has been cut by her, all other hairdressers have to do is follow her style. As for my color, I go to Christophe Robin on rue du Mont-Thabor.

What are your favorite beauty products?
Lots of love and a good face cream! I personally use Avène every day as well as Dior's apricot cream for my cuticles and nails.

Do you have a signature scent?
Any perfume from Guerlain, especially Mitsouko. I like the fact that you can't exactly decipher what composes these fragrances. They are harmonious and not aggressive.

What do you do for exercise?
Although I enjoy skiing and horseback riding, I don't really get a chance to do a lot of either. Mostly, my exercise comes from walking in the street, which I do quite often.

Lifestyle

How do you emphasize your personal style at home?

I used to prefer 17th century Swedish Gustavian style but now I believe that all beautiful things work together, whatever their epoch. Decoration depends on the house like fashion depends on the woman. For furniture, I recommend Objets Trouvés and for decoration and gift ideas, Galerie Sentou. Both are located in the Marais. Caravanne Chambre 19, on rue Saint Nicolas, is also charming for home furnishings.

Which are your favorite restaurants?

Angelina, on rue de Rivoli, is one of my favorite tearooms, along with Bread and Roses in the 6th arrondissement. I recommend Georges rue Mail for French cuisine and Orient Extrême for Asian food. I also enjoy receiving guests at home and find that the best food shopping in Paris is at the Bon Marché on rue de Sèvres.

Mina d'Ornano

I was at Chanel in Paris when the saleswoman told me about minaPoe, a new boutique she thought I should visit. I took her advice and instantly fell in love with it and with the designer and boutique owner, Mina d'Ornano. Of Slavic origin, Mina is a citizen of the world with a definite Parisian spirit. She began her career as an actress, then went on to become both a screenwriter and a director of her own plays. From writing to acting to designing, her passion has always been focused on style. When you walk into minaPoe, it feels like you are stepping into a cozy French boudoir. Her collections reflect a vintage style of bohemian luxury.

Personal style & style *philosophy*

Mina, as a designer of what could be considered haute couture accessories, what do you think defines French style and distinguishes it from others?

I think that in France women are psychologically freer. In certain countries, if a woman dresses too joyfully or uses too much color it makes her different, and this scares a lot of people. Here in France, women like and seek that difference. If from the start you don't care what people say, they get used to it. Then you are seen as a person who loves to dress up, who has interesting and unusual things. Actually, people love you for that. I think dressing is like an art: to each his own painting.

Everyone is different, especially if we look at other countries. The Italians are perfectly coordinated from head to toe, hair and make-up included. They are more "arranged" than French women whereas American women are more comfortable buying the whole outfit. What I find fun is making a match of non-matching things. One should enjoy one's clothes.

How would you define your personal style? Does anything influence it, such as fashion trends, or events in your life?

I have never followed trends and I have always enjoyed dressing up. When I was studying at the National Academy of Stage Drama in Paris, actor friends would compliment the vintage look I had created from pieces that I had found in the flea market. Now I do more serious vintage shopping, buying things such as 1930's dresses or Elizabethan tops that I mix with jeans. If I had to define my style I would say it's simply a mixture of styles, colors, seasons, and moods.

> *Even if I have 3 months* to prepare myself, *I always dress at the last minute.* It drives my husband crazy!

What in your opinion is the biggest fashion *faux pas*?
Someone who dresses purely for practicality, neglecting aestheticism and personality. The "total look" also falls into this category.

What is your favorite or signature look?
My favorite look is a perfectly cut pantsuit worn with high heels and a minaPoe scarf as an accessory. The accessory is the easy piece that can transform your whole outfit. A minaPoe brooch or scarf can have exactly the same effect as a piece of jewelry.

How do you dress for a last-minute special occasion?
Even if I have three months to prepare myself, I always dress at the last minute. It drives my husband crazy!

Fashion &
accessories

Which designer best reflects your personal style? I appreciate Jean Paul Gaultier because of his intelligent, unusual but wearable baroque style. He knows how to adapt, whether he is designing for pop stars or for Hermès. I also like the whimsical Japanese designer Tsumori Chisato, and Sabbia Rosa for its voluptuous and feminine lingerie.

What are your signature accessories? Do they change from day to night? Apart from my Eres lingerie, which has a fabulous quality and fit, I have a passion for shoes and often change them several times a day, for example, from hand-painted Converse sneakers to high heels. Shoes are no longer tied to a season. I love wearing boots in spring and high heel sandals in winter. The hardest thing is to find a nice pair of rain shoes but my black patent leather vintage Gucci clogs save me.

Who is your favorite shoe designer? Christian Louboutin's mini shoe boutique on rue Jean-Jacques Rousseau. It is so charming!

And for handbags? MinaPoe, of course! I'm always looking for the perfect handbag and personally try each one of my new models. A handbag should be luxurious, joyful, and practical.

What are your three must-have wardrobe pieces? My unique minaPoe fur coat, designed with Klimt motifs that go beautifully with both day and eveningwear, a pair of gold Manolo Blahnik boots that are timeless and go perfectly with nearly everything, and a black pleated skirt by Comme des Garçons that is original in cut and classic in color.

Is there an accessory you will never leave the house without? Yes, my watch. The notion of time is important to me, and given the frantic nature of my job, I need to keep track of it.

I love wearing *boots* *in spring* and high heel *sandals* *in winter...*

*The Joya Spa,
A heavenly
moment
of relaxation!*

Beauty

Who is your hairdresser of choice?
Massato, in Paris. After my hair has been cut, people constantly ask me who did it.

What are your favorite beauty products?
For my skin I use Sisley, the Crème Réparatrice, which never leaves my handbag, alternated with Sisleya and All Day All Year.

Which beauty treatment could you not do without?
Facials and skin care in general. I always use Sisley products: I use a mask and a scrub on a weekly basis. And when I need it, a ten-day, at-home Sisley botanical face treatment.

Do you have a signature scent?
I like to use Joy by Jean Patou, Eau du Soir by Sisley, and Acqua di Cologna from the pharmacy Santa Maria Novella in Florence.

What small personal pleasure do you treat yourself to occasionally?
The Joya Spa in the 8th arrondissement offers a foot reflexology massage followed by a pedicure. A heavenly moment of relaxation!

What do you do for exercise?
I swim, surf, ski, and do karate. In summer, I take advantage of the invigorating effect of the sea and waves. When I'm in Paris, I jog with my husband.

Lifestyle

Which are your favorite restaurants?

I always choose the quality of the cuisine first, but I like tiny, cozy cafés in small streets behind the Bastille or around Montmartre, the Café de Flore in Saint Germain-des-Près, and a lovely tearoom with a tiny conservatory in the 7th arrondissement near the Eiffel tower called Les Deux Abeilles. There are so many hidden places in Paris. Sometimes I like to simply get lost and wander parts of the city I don't know, certain of discovering new places full of charm.

T

Marie-Hélène de Taillac

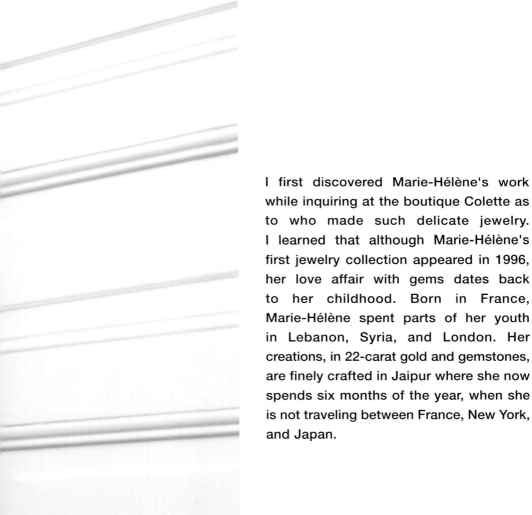

I first discovered Marie-Hélène's work while inquiring at the boutique Colette as to who made such delicate jewelry. I learned that although Marie-Hélène's first jewelry collection appeared in 1996, her love affair with gems dates back to her childhood. Born in France, Marie-Hélène spent parts of her youth in Lebanon, Syria, and London. Her creations, in 22-carat gold and gemstones, are finely crafted in Jaipur where she now spends six months of the year, when she is not traveling between France, New York, and Japan.

Personal style & style *philosophy*

Marie-Hélène, your multicultural background, international exposure, and sensitivity to color and materials have contributed to defining your personal style. As a French woman with Parisian flair, how would you define French style?
French women have their own style. In a way, they dress to seduce.

How would you define your personal style, and what outside influences impact your style sense?
I follow my personal instinct. If I were to describe that, I would say that it is contemporary chic but always comfortable.

Is there such a thing as good and bad taste when it comes to style? Someone with good taste will be wearing the right outfit at the right time whereas someone with poor taste will always look out of place and dressed for the wrong occasion. Someone chic fits into any situation.

What, in your opinion, is the biggest fashion *faux pas*?
The worst thing is to be dressed from head to toe in the same designer.

What is your signature look?
I have no shortage of clothes! Even at the last minute I can find something to wear.

"I have no shortage of clothes! Even at the *last minute* I can find something *to wear.*

I am not a buyer of "the bag of the season"

Be yourself and stay simple. Too many people dress to look something they are not versus dressing up *who they are.*

Fashion & *accessories*

Which designer best reflects your personal style?
Fashion is constantly changing so I don't choose one designer. However, I often wear Lucien Pellat-Finet sweaters because I like the sensuality of his creations.

What are your signature accessories? Do they change from day to night
My trademark is my jewelry. I wear the same, favorite pieces every day. At night, when I want to be dressier, I put on a necklace and change my bangles for more important bracelets.

What are your favorite handbag brands?
I am not a buyer of "the bag of the season", especially ones with logos, that will be out of fashion in six months time. I think they date too quickly. I prefer handbags that are unique in design.

What are your three must-have wardrobe pieces?
Beautiful lingerie that enhances the figure, great shoes, and, of course, jewelry.

What was your last great fashion discovery?
Martin Grant for evening wear and Miss Trish of Capri for flat sandals.

Are there any tips for having great style?
Be yourself and stay simple. Too many people dress to look like someone they are not instead of "dressing up" who they are.

Beauty

Who is your hairdresser of choice?
My son's hairdresser, Oscar by Simon.

What is your morning beauty ritual?
I usually put on Joelle Ciocco's aromatic lotion to wake up.

What are your favorite beauty products?
Joelle Ciocco, Dr. Hauschka, and Welleda products. They are all natural.

Do you have a signature scent, and does it change with the seasons?
The season doesn't impact my choice. I am loyal to Frédéric Malle.

What small personal pleasure do you treat yourself to occasionally?
An Ayurvedic body and face massage.

What is the best beauty advice you have been given?
To brush my teeth standing *on the tips of my toes.* It's a great way to keep the buttocks in shape.

EN PASSANT

Olivia Giacobetti

12 % PV - ALC 90°

What elements help create your personal ambiance at home?

Good food with good wine, subtle lighting, and beautiful flowers. Le Bon Marché is the best place for food shopping given the incredible choice, whereas Vertumne in the 1st arrondissement, makes the most wonderful bouquets. As for desserts, I believe that Gérard Mullot is the best address for pastries and bread.

..."Vertumne makes the most wonderful *bouquets*".

Do you have a preferred style of interior home design?

Contemporary design. I like things from Astier de Vilatte and from the Galerie Sentou.

Which are your favorite restaurants?

I prefer old-fashioned restaurants like Le Voltaire, Le Duc, and Le Récamier.

Spela Lenarcic

Hairdressers give you the best tips. My hairdresser, Mehdi Glaoua, introduced me to Spela. Born in Slovenia, Spela moved to Paris in 2000 to begin working as an assistant at French Vogue and for clients such as Ferragamo, Celine, Genny, and Roberto Cavalli. As a former consultant for Akris, she continues to work closely as a freelance stylist for prestigious international magazines. Some of her more recent commercial work includes Lancôme, Swarovski, and Hogan. Since 2005, her international "eye" has landed her the position of consultant for Celine.

Personal style & style *philosophy*

Spela, your profession requires you to feel, breathe, and live style. Now that Paris is your adopted home, what do you think defines French style and distinguishes it from others?

French style distinguishes itself from others by its femininity, timeless chic, and elegance. There is also an almost intellectual approach to its creativity and a moderate component of sexiness. Because sensuality is more important than sexuality, legs are a significant attribute. Italian style is sexier, more body-contouring, accessorized, and visible, given its important use of color and glitter. The Italian woman is more carnal in comparison to her French counterpart. As for American style, which apart from the Hollywood divas does not promote sexiness, its puritanical ways are sometimes expressed through sober cuts that are almost too perfect. Spanish style has a gothic-chic element to it, while English style balances classicism, extravagance, and creativity with taste. Compared to France, Japanese style is more infantile, less sophisticated, more brashly colored, and down-key on sex appeal.

> "French style distinguishes itself from others by its femininity, timeless chic and elegance,

How would you define your personal style? Does anything influence it, such as fashion trends or events in your life?
I would say that I embody the French definition of style complemented by a Slavic touch. My sensitivity towards style began when I was five years old and accompanied my mother to buy fabric for a dress in Slovenia. My arrival in Paris, at age 17, helped me fine-tune my personal style. Today, like many women, I love shoes and handbags.

Is there such a thing as good and bad taste when it comes to style?
For me, poor taste is a woman who no longer tries or dares to express her personal style. She has lost her curiosity and no longer cares about pleasing herself or others. On the other hand, good taste is all about charm, because beauty can also be vulgar.

What, in your opinion, is the biggest fashion faux pas?
Wearing the same outfit twice in a row. As a stylist, I often revert to the press offices, with whom I have strong relationships, to borrow clothes that are not yet in the boutiques.

What is your signature look?
A Dior Homme tuxedo pant suit in a small size, by Hedi Slimane, worn with a white shirt by Charvet, or Yves Saint Laurent, or even better, a 19th century vintage shirt found at Ragtime in Saint Germain-des-Près.

I love all designers

I like mixing vintage with Balenciaga, which fits me like a glove, wearing a studio creation by Givenchy...

Your favorite shoe brand
Pierre Hardy

Fashion & *accessories*

Which designer best reflects your personal style? I love all designers. I like mixing vintage with Balenciaga, which fits me like a glove, wearing a studio creation by Givenchy, or getting dressed in Celine when I want a more sport-chic, easy-to-wear look.

What are your signature accessories? Do they change from day to night?
There are, of course, the must-haves we all know, by Hermès and Louis Vuitton. In this domain, where certain models resemble each other, it is ultimately quality that is sought out and paid for.

Who is your favorite handbag designer?
That depends on the season. I would say Givenchy, Yves Saint Laurent by Stefano Pilati, and Celine by Ivana Omazic. However, my favorite handbag of all, is a wool and wooden one that I found in Ljubljana, Slovenia.

What are your must-have wardrobe pieces?
My black coat from Viktor & Rolf with balloon sleeves, tapered waist-line and removable lining, the new Levis 511 jean by Levis Strauss, a vinyl and goatskin jacket by Balenciaga, and a vintage handbag.

What was your last great fashion discovery?
Color. Although it may be easier to achieve elegance wearing black, grey, brown, or white, it is quite a different story when dealing with color. As a stylist, I have always known how to work color for others but have only recently started using it more for myself.

Are there any tips for having great style? Wear black if you are a bit robust. Rely on the expertise of a professional stylist who can help you enhance your personal style if you feel unsure and most importantly, respect yourself.

Beauty

Who is your hairdresser of choice?
Orlando Pita for his studio work, Rudolph Farmer for his youth and talent, and Mehdi Glaoua for the magic cut. I also love Max Delorme for make-up.

What is your morning beauty ritual?
I start off the day by splashing my face with cold water.

What are your favorite beauty products?
Omega-3 fluid anti-irritation cream by Sonya Dakar, L.A., California.

Which aspects of your health-beauty regime could you not live without?
Minancora cream from Brazil.

Do you have a signature scent?
Annick Goutal, because I find that this perfumer focuses on pure and natural scents, versus the heavier chemical scents of most other perfumers.

What small, personal pleasure do you treat yourself to occasionally?
A Chinese massage by Mr. François Liu. Extraordinary!

What is the best beauty advice you have been given?
Sleep.

Lifestyle

Which are your favorite restaurants?
Brasserie : Au Chien qui Fume,
French : Bistrot de Paris,
Italian : Da Mimmo and Café Peonia,
Argentinean : Anahi,
Japanese : Yamamoto

Carole
Rochas

I met Carole at her apartment on the rue de l'Université where she makes beautiful one-of-a kind jewelry pieces for private clients only. She is a ravishing, blonde, sexy, cultured, delightful woman with the tiniest waist I have ever seen. She told me she walks everywhere in flat shoes, but carries her heels to change into if she has an appointment. We spent the afternoon having tea in her cozy apartment, and after our meeting she invited me to dinner. Our meeting ended at 6:00 pm and dinner was at 9:00. Carole managed to cook a three-course dinner of *risotto*, *gigot d'agneau*, and *tarte aux pommes*, set the table, change her clothes, and be ready for her guests in plenty of time.

Personal style & style *philosophy*

Carole, as a woman of many talents, with an educated eye and a true sensitivity for aesthetics, what do you think defines French style and distinguishes it from others?

I don't really think there is a "French" style. With the influence of the media and the opening of borders, you find the same clothes everywhere. What makes the difference is cultural: the way of life, the climate, the education. All of these things mean that American, Russian, Italian, or French women are going to wear the same clothes but each will have a different "look." Jeans have become the global uniform. Times have changed. People don't live the way they used to.

How would you define your personal style? Does anything influence it, such as fashion trends, or events in your life?

I dress in a fairly classic style with what I hope are touches of originality. I had the good fortune of seeing my mother in fabulous clothes from Balenciaga, Philippe Venet, and Madame Grès, and of seeing my mother-in-law always perfectly dressed by Yves Saint Laurent, so you could say that my eye received a good education. That said, I believe that elegance is possible only if one is in harmony with oneself. If you are comfortable with who you are, you look better in your clothes. Good taste is harmony: harmony of shapes, of colors, and of knowing what looks good on you.

"I think bad taste is *wanting to be* too fashionable...

Is there such a thing as good and bad taste when it comes to style?
I think bad taste is wanting to be too "fashionable," accumulating too many brands, and wanting to look like someone you are not.

What is your signature look?
I would choose a straight, black skirt with a high waist and a fine black cashmere cardigan that I would button down the back and wear over a lace corset by Cadolle. I'd also wear sheer black stockings and very high black pumps by Gucci. One piece of advice would be to adapt yourself to your body type and your natural colors.

How do you dress for a last-minute special event?
The ideal last-minute outfit is an Yves Saint Laurent tuxedo with a skirt or pants and a black sweater or a blouse, with more or less jewelry, depending on the occasion.

You can wear the same piece of clothing for day and evening simply by **changing accessories**

Carole Rochas

Fashion &
accessories

Which designer most reflects your personal style?
During the day, I almost never wear dresses, rather a straight skirt with a sweater, or a blouse and jacket. If I have to be a little dressier, I wear a Chanel suit, always with the famous two-toned beige and black shoes. During the summer, I'm often in jeans with a T-shirt or blouse and blazer, or in a sweater with a tweed jacket in the winter.
For the evening, Yves Saint Laurent has created divine dresses. Jean Paul Gaultier has incredible talent, and Christian Lacroix is a magician born to create costumes for the stage. When will there be a "Traviata" for which he will do the wardrobe? Personally, I wear Madame Grès vintage dresses, which I find sublime.

What are your signature accessories? Do they change from day to night? I don't look for brands. What I love, for example, is going to Zara where you can always find gorgeous things: sweaters, blouses, shoes, and coats. I've also discovered beautiful, well-cut, soft sweaters at Mango. You can wear the same piece of clothing for either day or evening by simply changing your accessories, especially jewelry. I've created jewelry in light wood for the day and in ebony, diamonds, and pearls for the evening.

Who is your favorite shoe designer?
I love Manolo Blahnik's shoes, especially for the evening. For the daytime, Delage makes pretty, comfortable shoes.

And for handbags?
I have a collection of bags by Renaud Pellegrino. Otherwise, I'm crazy about Asian baskets from Indonesia and Japan, and I'm quite fond of the Hermès Birkin bag.

Beauty

Who is your hairdresser of choice?
I never go to the hairdresser. If I want a good banana up-do, I call Christophe Rosso, who comes to the house. I almost always have my hair back in a rubber band or a barrette. I love really short hair, like Sharon Stone used to have, but I would never dare cut mine.

What is your morning beauty ritual? After I awaken, I brush my hair, use Avène spray on my face, and then brush my teeth. Voilà!

What are you favorite beauty products?
Elizabeth Arden's 8 Hour Cream has been a part of my life since my childhood for lips and any irritation. I take off my make-up with hazelnut oil. Before I put my make-up on, I use Estée Lauder's Idealist, then Pearl Veil by Terry and a light foundation by Gemey. For evening, I use orchid powder from LeClerc and a rose blush. I would have a hard time doing without the 8 Hour Cream or mascara, but I think that ultimately the best beauty product is love. A dazzling effect is virtually assured!

Which beauty treatment could you not do without?
It's a true joy to have a weekly massage at home, and if I can do a steam bath and body peel beforehand, it's a dream! The best beauty and health advice that I've been given is no sun... although I don't always follow it.

Do you have a signature scent? I have the good fortune to have a friend who has made a wonderful tuberose extract for years. I am totally loyal.

What do you do for exercise? As I don't drive, I go everywhere on foot. I also try to do five minutes of little exercises a day for my arms and abs.

The best beauty and *health advice* that I've been given is no sun... although I don't always *follow it.*

Lifestyle

How do you emphasize your style at home?

From interior design to clothes, the best style is adaptation. There has to be harmony. A house by the ocean shouldn't be decorated like a chalet or an apartment in town. I love to decorate but if I had to choose a decorator, it would be Alberto Pinto, who does extraordinary houses down to the smallest detail: sheets, plates, etc. In terms of rare paintings, Waring Hopkins is surely the best of advisors. I also like to go to J.G. Mitterand's gallery to discover talented artists and to the studio of Anilore Banon, who creates superb furniture, such as tables and chairs, that resemble sculptures.

What elements help create your personal ambiance at home?

All year round, my patios stay green. In the house, I love to have orchids in Japanese pots and antique Asian baskets. I also like scented candles, tuberose in summer, potpourri in winter, and orange peel, cedar, and amber oils for burning on lamps.

In your home, which is the most important room for you and why?

I spend most of my time in my bedroom, as that's where I create my jewelry.
I've just redecorated it in an exotic Chinese style that makes me feel good and inspires me.

Which are your favorite restaurants?

I like to go to Le Récamier where you can order soufflés and the best *pot-au-feu* in Paris. When the weather is nice and warm, the absolute luxury is to go to Laurent for the spider crab in aspic, and crispy *langoustines*-a real treat! I also like the real bistros, like Georges, Le Pré Cadet or l'Ami Jean, and the Italian restaurant Le Perron, where the thin, *tagliatelle* with seasonal white truffles is exquisite!

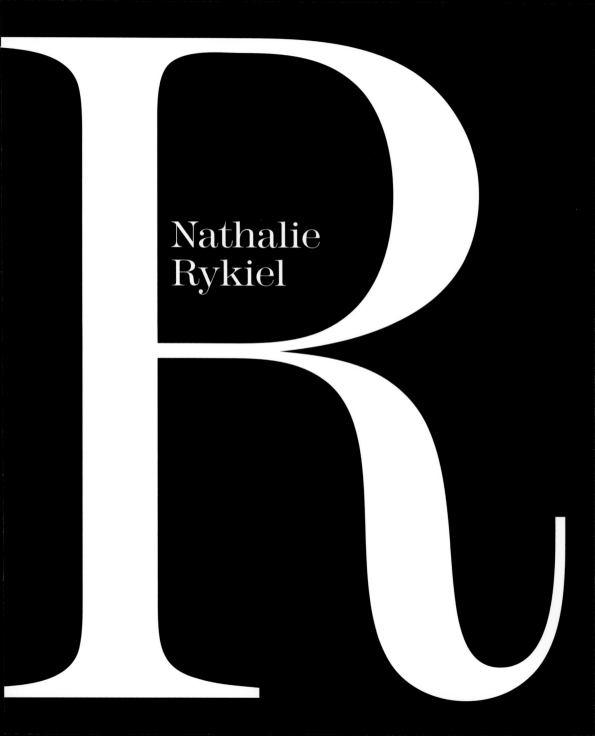

Nathalie
Rykiel

While meandering down the rue de Grenelle, one of my favorite streets on the Left Bank, I stumbled upon a boutique called Rykiel Woman. The name intrigued me. I discovered it had been created by Nathalie Rykiel, daughter of the legendary French fashion designer Sonia Rykiel. Rykiel Woman is a lingerie boutique, but not just for bras and underwear. It carries luxurious boudoir attire: fur vests, cashmere bed clothes, and "pleasure" toys presented, *naturellement*, with panache and style. I met Nathalie in her office last summer. She was wearing a T-shirt that said "Blonde." Nathalie is a brunette. She likes to shock.

Personal style & style *philosophy*

Nathalie, you began modeling for Sonia Rykiel when you were 20 years old. After this experience, you invested yourself in the business from a managerial perspective. Over the years, you have created new lines as well as numerous fragances for the Rykiel brand. Today, you are the Artistic Director. After all this experience and exposure in the fashion world, both professionally and personally, what, in your opinion, defines French style and distinguishes it from others?

The French woman is not afraid of being different from the others. French style is about having a personal attitude that mixes self-confidence and allure, as well as individuality. It's also about seduction and sensuality without ostentation.

How would you define your personal style? Does anything influence it, such as fashion trends, or events in your life?

My personal style reflects my evolution, education, culture, and life as a woman. What matters to me is to feel great and confident in my clothes. Once I've found something that suits me, I can wear it every day.

Is there such a thing as good and bad taste when it comes to style? I believe taste is completely subjective, and I deny anyone the right to decree what is in good or bad taste. What I consider good taste, the person next to me might consider bad taste.

What, in your opinion, is the biggest fashion *faux pas*? Not feeling good about yourself, or wearing something trendy that doesn't suit you.

What is your signature look? A pair of jeans, high heels, a large belt, a Rykiel sweater, and incredible antique jewelery.

How do you dress for a last-minute special occasion? If I don't have time to change, I would freshen my make-up, have my hair done, and probably add jewels and accessories to my clothes.

> "My personal style reflects my evolution, education, culture and life as a woman."

Fashion & accessories

Which designer most reflects your personal style?
Sonia Rykiel's dresses are timeless and ultra feminine.

What are your signature accessories? Do they change from day to night?
With Rykiel and Prada, you can't make mistakes. You can wear them day or night. Great shoes are always a plus!

Who is your favorite shoe designer
Rykiel and Christian Louboutin.

And for handbags? Sonia Rykiel, Jamin Puech, Marni, and Prada.

What was your last great fashion discovery?
A great pair of jeans by Gold Sign that I found at L'Eclaireur.

Are there any tips for having great style?
As Cocteau said, *"Ce que le public te reproche, cultive-le, c'est toi."* Which means, "Cultivate what the public criticizes about you, as that is you." In other words, be yourself.

"What the public criticizes you for, cultivate it because it's you" *Jean Cocteau*

elle aime

With *Rykiel* & *Prada*, you can't make mistakes.

*I only wear Rykiel Woman
by Sonia Rykiel whether it
is morning or evening, summer
or winter. I don't care.*

Beauty

Who is your hairdresser of choice? Christophe Robin.

What is your morning beauty ritual? I drink a large glass of water.

What are your favorite beauty products?
Lait-Crème Concentré by Embryolisse, Eau Démaquillante for face and eyes by Make Up For Ever, jasmine mask for hair by Leonor Greyl, shampoo Bain Satin N°2 by Kérastase, as well as Evian's face spray, Stéphane Marais' black mascara comb, and African body cream by Omoyé.

Which beauty treatment could you not do without? I love to get a manicure and pedicure every week. I always wear red nail polish on my feet.

What small personal pleasure do you treat yourself to occasionally?
When I can, I love to get massaged at home by a fantastic Japanese woman. Sometimes I also go to the Turkish baths at the Ritz.

What is the best beauty advice you have been given?
Look at yourself in the mirror, alone, without girlfriends, daughters, husband or lovers and be objective with yourself. Look at what's "good" and learn to emphazise it in the best way you can. Then, look at what is "not so good" and try to hide it in the best way possible. Have fun with it, and most importantly, love yourself.

What do you do for exercise?
Pilates twice a week, and power plate at Elements.

Lifestyle

How do you emphasize your style at home?

My home is not a showroom. It's a family place, with a sense of harmony, pleasure, and beauty, where I raise my children. I love to mix comfort and beauty. The comfort of armchairs and sofas is a priority.

What elements help create your personal ambiance ?

I love fresh flowers in small vases, and place them everywhere throughout the house. I light scented candles in the evening as soon as I arrive home, and always light a fire in the chimney during winter. Because lighting is very important, I have dimmer switches on almost every lamp in the house, and there are always big fruit and vegetable baskets in the kitchen.

In your home, which is the most important room for you and why ?

I have two favorite rooms. Firstly, my bedroom because I love doing everything from my bed, such as making phone calls, watching TV, or reading magazines and books. I can work, read, eat, make love, or rest with a lot of pleasure. Secondly, my kitchen because it's the heart of the house, a place where everybody meets and shares meals. It's an essential room for the family.

Which are your favorite restaurants?

La Maison du Caviar, Hôtel Costes restaurant, Le Stresa, Cafe de Flore, and Davé.

Le Stresa

addresses

A

Alexandre Zouari
1 av. du Président-Wilson - 75016 Paris
Tel 01 47 23 79 00

L'Ami Jean
27 rue Malar - 75007 Paris
Tel 01 47 05 86 89

Alberto Pinto
11 rue d'Aboukir - 75002 Paris
Tel 01 40 13 00 00

Anaconda Atelier
16 rue des Saints-Pères - 75007 Paris
Tel 01 42 60 18 29

Anahi
49 rue Volta - 75003 Paris
Tel 01 48 87 88 24

Angelina
226 rue de Rivoli - 75001 Paris
Tel 01 42 60 82 00

Anilore Banon
7 rue de Nantes - 75019 Paris
Tel 01 42 05 24 22

Annick Goutal
14 rue de Castiglione - 75001 Paris
Tel 01 42 60 52 82
Other boutiques in Paris.

L'Assiette
181 rue du Château - 75014 Paris
Tel 01 43 22 64 86

Astier de Villatte
173 rue Saint-Honoré - 75001 Paris
Tel 01 43 45 72 72

Au Chien qui Fume
33 rue du Pont-Neuf - 75001 Paris
Tel 01 42 36 07 42

B

Balenciaga
10 av. George-V - 75008 Paris
Tel 01 47 20 21 11

Barboza
356 rue Saint-Honoré - 75001 Paris
Tel 01 42 60 67 08

Bistrot de Paris
33 rue de Lille - 75007 Paris
Tel 01 42 61 15 84

Bonbino
Carrousel du Louvre, 99 rue de Rivoli,
75001 Paris

Le Bon Marché
24 rue de Sèvres - 75007 Paris
Tel 01 44 39 80 00

Bread and Roses
62 rue Madame - 75006 Paris
Tel 01 42 22 06 06

By Terry
21 et 36 passage Véro-Dodat
75007 Paris - Tel 01 44 76 00 76
Other boutiques in Paris.

Cadolle
255 rue Saint-Honoré - 75001 Paris
Tel 01 42 60 94 94

Café de Flore
172 bd Saint-Germain - 75006 Paris
Tel 01 45 48 55 26

Café Peonia
153 rue de Billancourt - 92100 Boulogne
Tel 01 46 04 65 23

Caravane Chambre 19
19 rue Saint-Nicolas - 75012 Paris
Tel 01 53 02 96 96

Caudalie
Espace Bien-Être Caudalie
Le Meurice, 228 rue de Rivoli
75001 Paris - Tel 01 44 58 10 77

Carole Rochas
By appointment with Susan Tabak
Tel (+1) 212 404 8398

Celine
36 av. Montaigne - 75008 Paris
Tel 01 56 89 07 92
Other boutiques in Paris.

Chanel
31 rue Cambon - 75001 Paris
Tel 01 42 86 26 00
Other boutiques in Paris.

Charvet
28 place Vendôme - 75001 Paris
Tel 01 42 60 30 70

Chloé
44 av. Montaigne - 75008 Paris
Tel 01 47 23 00 08
Other boutiques in Paris.

Christian Louboutin
19 rue Jean-Jacques Rousseau
75001 Paris - Tel 01 42 36 05 31

38 rue de Grenelle - 75007 Paris
Tel 01 42 22 33 07

Christophe Rosso
By appointment
Tel 06 07 89 18 44

Colette
213 rue Saint-Honoré - 75001 Paris
Tel 01 55 35 33 90

Coloriste Christophe Robin
7 rue du Mont-Thabor - 75001 Paris
Tel 01 42 60 99 15

Comme des Garçons
54 rue du Fbg Saint-Honoré
75008 Paris - Tel 01 53 30 27 27
Other boutiques in Paris.

D

Da Mimmo
39 rue Magenta - 75010 Paris
Tel 01 42 06 44 47

Davé
12 rue de Richelieu - 75001 Paris
Tel 01 42 61 49 48

Delage
159 galerie de Valois,
Jardins du Palais Royal - 75001 Paris
Tel 01 40 15 97 24

Les Deux Abeilles
189 rue de l'Université - 75007 Paris
Tel 01 45 55 64 04

Dior
30 av. Montaigne - 75008 Paris
Tel 01 40 73 73 73
Other boutiques in Paris.

Dior Jewellery
8 place Vendôme - 75001 Paris
Tel 01 42 96 30 84
Other boutiques in Paris.

Diptyque
34 bd Saint-Germain - 75006 Paris
Tel 01 43 26 45 27
Other boutiques in Paris.

Le Dôme
108 bd du Montparnasse
75014 Paris - Tel 01 43 35 25 81

Le Duc
243 bd Raspail - 75014 Paris
Tel 01 43 22 59 59

E

L'Eclaireur
3ter rue des Rosiers - 75004 Paris
Tel 01 48 87 10 22
Other boutiques in Paris.

Eléments
41 rue de Richelieu - 75001 Paris
Tel 01 40 20 42 62

Eres
2 rue Tronchet - 75008 Paris
Tel 01 47 42 28 82
Other boutiques in Paris.

F

Fendi
24 rue François Ier - 75008 Paris
Tel 01 49 52 84 52

Forum Diffusion
55 rue Pierre-Demours - 75017 Paris
Tel 01 43 80 87 00

François Liu
5 rue Muller - 75018 Paris
Tel 01 42 52 87 86

Frédérique Malle
21 rue du Mont-Thabor
75001 Paris - Tel 01 42 22 77 22
Other boutiques in Paris.

Galerie Sentou
18 and 24 rue du Pont-Louis Philippe
75004 Paris - Tel 01 42 77 44 79
Other galeries in Paris.

Galignani
224 rue de Rivoli - 75001 Paris
Tel 01 42 60 76 07

Georgina Brandolini
16 bd Raspail - 75006 Paris
Tel 01 45 44 27 96

Gérard Mulot
76 rue de Seine - 75006 Paris
Tel 01 43 26 85 77
Other boutiques in Paris.

Chez Georges
1 rue du Mail - 75002 Paris
Tel 01 42 60 07 11

Gisele So
50 rue de Sèvres - 75007 Paris
Tel 01 43 06 37 79

Givenchy
56 rue François Ier - 75008 Paris
Tel 01 40 76 07 27
Other boutiques in Paris.

La Grande Epicerie
38 rue de Sèvres - 75007 Paris
Tel 01 44 39 81 00

Gucci
2 rue du Fbg Saint-Honoré
75008 Paris - Tel 01 44 94 14 70
Other boutiques in Paris.

Guerlain
68 av. des Champs-Elysées
75008 Paris - Tel 01 45 62 52 57
Other boutiques in Paris.

Hôtel Costes
239 rue Saint-Honoré - 75001 Paris
Tel 01 42 44 50 00

Hôtel Le Bristol
112 rue du Fbg Saint-Honoré
75008 Paris - Tel 01 53 43 43 00

Hôtel Plaza Athenée
25 av. Montaigne - 75008 Paris
Tel 01 53 67 66 65

Hôtel Ritz
15 place Vendôme - 75001 Paris
Tel 01 43 16 30 30

Hermès
24 rue du Fbg Saint-Honoré,
75008 Paris - Tel 01 40 17 47 17
Other boutiques in Paris.

Hopkins Custot Galerie
2 av. Matignon - 75008 Paris
Tel 01 42 25 32 32

La Hune
170 bd Saint-Germain,
75006 Paris - Tel 01 45 48 35 85

J

J. G. M Galerie
79 rue du Temple - 75003 Paris
Tel 01 43 26 12 05

Jamin Puech
68 rue Vieille-du-Temple
75003 Paris - Tel 01 48 87 84 87
Other boutiques in Paris.

Jean Patou
5 rue de Castiglione - 75001 Paris
Tel 01 42 92 07 22

Jean Paul Gaultier
44 av. Georges V - 75008 Paris
Tel 01 44 43 00 44
Other boutiques in Paris.

Joelle Ciocco
8 place de la Madeleine - 75008 Paris
Tel 01 42 60 58 80

Joya
6 rue de la Renaissance - 75008 Paris
Tel 01 40 70 16 49

K

Kabuki
21 rue Etienne-Marcel
75001 Paris - Tel 01 42 33 13 44
Other boutiques in Paris. ·

Katia & Valentin
By appointment
Tel 06 08 65 86 01

L

Laurent
41 av. Gabriel - 75008 Paris
Tel 01 42 25 00 39

Le Jour et l'Heure
6 rue du Dragon - 75006 Paris
Tel 01 42 22 96 11

Louis Vuitton
101 av. des Champs-Elysées
75008 Paris - Tel 01 53 57 24 00
Other boutiques in Paris.

Loulou de la Falaise
7 rue de Bourgogne - 75007 Paris
Tel 01 45 51 42 22

21 rue Cambon - 75001
Tel 01 42 60 02 66

Lucien Pellat-Finet
1 rue Montalembert - 75007 Paris
Tel 01 42 22 22 77

La Maison du Caviar
21 rue Quentin Bauchart - 75008 Paris
Tel 01 47 23 53 43

Manolo Blahnik
Maria Luisa
40 rue du Mont-Thabor - 75001 Paris
Tel 01 47 03 48 08

Marco Matysik
Colette
213 rue Saint-Honoré - 75001 Paris
Tel 01 55 35 33 90

Marché aux Puces de Clignancourt
75018 Paris (Saturday - Monday)

Marianne Robic
39 rue de Babylone - 75007 Paris
Tel 01 53 63 14 00

Marie-Hélène de Taillac
8 rue de Tournon - 75006 Paris
Tel 01 44 27 07 07

Marni
57 av. Montaigne - 75008 Paris
Tel 01 56 88 08 08

Martin Grant
10 rue Charlot - 75003 Paris
Tel 01 42 71 39 49

Massato
5 rue Volney - 75002 Paris
Tel 01 42 96 10 04
Other boutiques in Paris.

Le Mathis
3 rue de Ponthieu - 75008 Paris
Tel 01 53 76 39 55

Max Delorme
9 rue de la Paix - 75001 Paris
Tel 01 55 35 35 00

Mehdi Glaoua
By appointment.
Tel 06 13 50 79 72.

minaPoe
19 rue Duphot - 75001 Paris
Tel 01 42 61 06 41

Miu Miu
16 rue de Grenelle - 75007 Paris
Tel 01 53 63 20 30

Moulié
8 place du Palais-Bourbon
75007 Paris - Tel 01 45 51 78 43

Le Moulin à Vent
20 rue des Fossés Saint-Bernard
75005 Paris - Tel 01 43 54 99 37

Nuxe Spa Montorgueil
32 rue Montorgueil - 75001 Paris
Tel 01 55 80 71 40

Objets Trouvés
25 rue Saint-Paul - 75004 Paris
Tel 01 48 04 04 42

Olivier Pitou
23 rue des Saints-Pères
75006 Paris - Tel 01 49 27 97 49

Orient-Extrême
4 rue Bernard-Palissy
75006 Paris - Tel 01 44 39 80 00

Orlando Pita
Call Callisté (Tel 01 40 26 76 77)
Ask Jean-François Raffalli

Oscar by Simon
16 rue Vavin
75006 Paris - Tel 01 53 10 08 12

P

Le Perron
6 rue Perronet, 75007 Paris
Tel 01 45 44 71 51

Poilâne
8 rue du Cherche-Midi - 75006 Paris
Tel 01 45 48 42 59

Pierre Hardy
156 galerie de Valois, Jardins du Palais
Royal - 75001 Paris - Tel 01 42 60 59 75

Prada
10 av. Montaigne
75008 Paris
Tel 01 53 23 99 40
Other boutiques in Paris.

Le Pré Cadet
10 rue Saulnier - 75009 Paris
Tel 01 48 24 99 64

R

Ragtime
23 rue de l'Echaudé
75006 Paris
Tel 01 56 24 00 36

Le Récamier La Cigale
4 rue Récamier - 75007 Paris
Tel 01 45 48 86 58

Le Relais de l'Entrecôte
20^(bis) rue Saint-Benoît
75006 Paris
Tel 01 45 49 16 00
Other restaurant in Paris.

Le Relais Paza
21 av. Montaigne - 75008 Paris
Tel 01 53 67 64 00

Renaud Pellegrino
14 rue du Fbg Saint-Honoré
75008 Paris - Tel 01 42 65 35 52

Roger Vivier
29 rue du Fbg Saint-Honoré
75008 Paris - Tel 01 53 43 00 85

Rykiel Woman
6 rue de Grenelle - 75007 Paris
Tel 01 49 54 66 21

Sabbia Rosa
73 rue des Saints-Pères
75006 Paris - Tel 01 45 48 88 37

Sephora
70 av. des Champs-Elysées
75008 Paris - Tel 01 53 93 22 50

Shu Uemura
176 bd Saint Germain - 75006 Paris
Tel 01 45 48 02 55

Simone
1 rue Saint-Simon - 75007 Paris
Tel 01 42 22 81 40

Sisley
1 rue du Four - 75006 Paris
Tel 01 43 29 14 22

Sonia Rykiel
175 bd Saint-Germain - 75006 Paris
Tel 01 49 54 60 60

Le Stresa
7 rue Chambiges - 75008 Paris
Tel 01 47 23 51 62

Tsumori Chisato
20 rue Barbette - 75003 Paris
Tel 01 42 78 18 88

Valentino
17 av. Montaigne - 75008 Paris
Tel 01 47 23 64 61
Other boutiques in Paris.

Vanessa Bruno
12 rue de Castiglione - 75001 Paris
Tel 01 42 61 44 60
Other boutiques in Paris.

Vertumne
12 rue de la Sourdière - 75001 Paris
Tel 01 42 86 06 76

Viktor & Rolf
Colette
213 rue Saint-Honoré - 75001 Paris
Tel 01 55 35 33 90

Le Voltaire
27 quai Voltaire - 75007 Paris
Tel 01 42 61 17 49

Y

Yamamoto
6 rue Chabannais - 75002 Paris
Tel 01 49 27 97 26

Yves Saint Laurent
38 rue du Fbg Saint-Honoré
75008 Paris.
Tel 01 42 65 74 59
Other boutiques in Paris.

Z

Zadig et Voltaire
15 rue du Jour - 75001 Paris
Tel 01 42 21 88 70
Other boutiques in Paris.

Zara
39 bd Haussmann - 75009 Paris
Tel 01 40 98 00 03
Other boutiques in Paris.

About the author

With her fluent French and close friendships with even the hardest-to-crack boutique owners, style-setters, and merchandise gatekeepers, author Susan Tabak has gained *entrée* to Paris secrets known to only a select few. Susan's love for France was evident from the first time she arrived in the country.

The Paris Personal Shopper vision first developed while Susan was on vacation with family and friends. One friend was so impressed by Susan's use of the language, she suggested they continue to travel together so Susan could help break down the cultural barriers. This incident sparked the realization that Susan could use her fluent French and extensive knowledge of the city of Paris to form a business.

Launched in 2001, Paris Personal Shopper incorporates Susan's love and knowledge of Paris and shopping. The company's primary focus is to provide customized shopping excursions in the fashion capital of the world. Susan prepares an extensive itinerary, based on the needs and goals of her clients, and then accompanies them to the most fabulous neighborhoods and shops around Paris to help them find their desired wardrobe pieces.

Susan currently resides in New York City with her husband and three children.

Thanks to...

There are many people I would like to thank for helping me formulate the vision for this book. In particular, I am grateful to my amazing, energetic, and enthusiastic team: Ambroise Tézenas, my talented and forever optimistic photographer who put the team together; Anne Senechal, my persevering and dilligent production manager; Julie Cheroy, my creative graphic artist; Hilary Reyl for her help with translation; Shelley Lewis for her editorial skills and keen eye; and Sharyn Kolberg for her assistance in crafting the words and phraseology.

To all 8 fabulous women, who took time out of their busy schedules to be interviewed and photographed, and to Laura Ungaro and Jean-Gabriel Mitterrand for their thoughtfulness and generosity on this project.

To my friends: Simonetta Speri for her wise ideas, outstanding organizational abilities and true friendship; Shelley Aarons for her unyielding inspiration which led me to establish Paris Personal Shopper; Oz Garcia for insisting that I write this book; and Jolie Stahl for her artistic flair and critical eye.

To my family: My children Alexis, Elizabeth and Philip for their patience and understanding and my husband Jeffrey for his relentless support and encouragement.

And last but not least, to Paris for all the joy and inspiration that it has given me throughout the years.

Susan Tabak

Paris Personal Shopper

www. parispersonalshopper.com

Email: susan@parispersonalshopper.com

Tel: 212 404 8398

A Seline Edition, First printing 2006 - ISBN: 0-9779964-0-9